WEATHER OR NOT

Riddles for Rain and Shine

by Rick & Ann Walton
pictures by Susan Slattery Burke

 Lerner Publica

...neapolis

This and the last five to Alan, who brightens our every day   —R.W. & A.W.

To my brother, Pat, for his sunny voice on the phone every morning   —S.S.B

Copyright © 1990 by Lerner Publications Company

This book is available in two editions:
Library binding by Lerner Publications Company
Soft cover by First Avenue Editions
241 First Avenue North
Minneapolis, Minnesota 55401

Library of Congress Cataloging-in-Publication Data

Walton, Rick
  Weather or not: riddles for rain and shine/by Rick & Ann Walton; pictures
by Susan Slattery Burke.
     p.   cm.—(You must be joking)
  Summary: A collection of riddles about weather, including "What do clouds
wear under their raincoats? Thunderwear."
  ISBN 0-8225-2329-9 (lib. bdg.)
  ISBN 0-8225-9580-X (pbk.)
  1. Riddles, Juvenile. 2. Rain and rainfall—Juvenile humor. [1. Weather—
Wit and humor. 2. Riddles.] I. Walton, Ann, 1963-   . II. Burke, Susan Slattery,
ill. III. Title. IV. Series.
PN6371.5.W37   1990
398.6—dc20   89-36628
                                                                  CIP
                                                                   AC
Manufactured in the United States of America

    2 3 4 5 6 7 8 9 10 99 98 97 96 95 94 93 92 91

Q: What do snowmen ride?

A: Ice-cycles.

Q: What kind of salad do snowmen eat?
A: Coldslaw.

Q: What do snowmen put on their faces
to keep them looking young?
A: Cold cream.

Q: What do snowmen put on their faces
to keep them looking even younger?
A: Ice cream.

Q: Why are snowmen careful not to get into trouble?

A: Because they don't want to be in hot water.

Q: What do woodcutters do when all the trees freeze?

A: They wait for a good thaw.

Q: What likes to graze, lie in the sun, and dump two feet of snow on unsuspecting towns?

A: A bull-lizard.

Q: Where are cold temperatures made?

A: In wind chill factories.

Q: What did the sun say to the snowman?

A: "I thaw you!"

Q: What do well-dressed snowmen wear?

A: Snowsuits.

Q: Where should you keep a snowstorm?
A: In cold storage.

Q: How do you know when a snowstorm is saying goodbye?
A: You can see a cold wave.

Q: What should you wear if you want to go out in a hailstorm?
A: A hailmet.

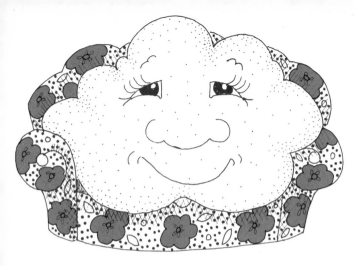

Q: What do clouds sit on?
A: Air cushions.

Q: What do clouds wear when it gets cold?
A: Raincoats.

Q: What do clouds wear under their raincoats?
A: Thunderwear.

Q: How do you buy a cloud?
A: With a rain check.

Q: Where should you keep your clouds?
A: In a cloud bank.

Q: Why shouldn't you wear
snowshoes?
A: Because they'll melt.

Q: What's the weather always like at parades?

A: Partly crowdy.

Q: How do clouds know where they're supposed to go?

A: They look at a weather map.

Q: How do you lock a storm door?

A: With a thunderbolt.

Q: Why does lightning never go twice to the same bowling alley?

A: Because lightning never strikes twice in the same place.

Q: Where can you buy a storm?
A: From a storm cellar.

Q: When is it unsafe to walk in the rain?
A: When it's raining cats and dogs.

Q: How can you tell if it's going to rain cats and dogs?

A: The wind will begin to howl.

Q: How do you know when it's raining cats and dogs?

A: You can see all the poodles.

Q: What's the temperature like when it rains cats and dogs?

A: It's biting cold.

Q: What's stranger than when it rains cats and dogs?

A: When kings rain.

Q: What's even stranger than kings raining?
A: Baby showers.

Q: When is the earth cleanest?

A: Right after it showers.

Q: What's the best way to keep from getting wet when you go outside?

A: Don't go out when it's raining.

Q: What do you get when a cloudburst hits a flock of ducks?

A: A downpour.

Q: Why doesn't Mother Nature cover the grass in water every morning?

A: She doesn't want to over-dew it.

Q: What does the sun drink out of?

A: Sunglasses.

Q: What does the sun eat off of?

A: A hot plate.

Q: Why is the sun a welcome guest at parties?

A: Because the sun knows how to break the ice.

Q: What do you get when you cross the sun with a goose?

A: Sundown.

Q: How do you hold up the sky during the daytime?

A: With sunbeams.

Q: Why is the sun so bright?

A: Because it has millions of degrees.

Q: What makes a cloudburst?
A: A windbreaker.

Q: When do you know that the weather's sad?
A: When you hear the wind wailing.

Q: Where should you keep the wind?
A: In an air pocket.

Q: What's the best way to shoot the breeze?
A: With an air rifle.

Q: What does the breeze blow?

A: Wind instruments.

Q: What are clouds' favorite wind instruments?

A: Foghorns.

Q: How do you protect yourself from an angry windstorm?

A: With a windshield.

Q: Who saves clouds from danger?
A: Thunderdog.

Q: Why is thunder so noisy?
A: Because it uses a cloudspeaker.

Q: How did the first person ever hit by lightning feel?
A: Shocked.

Q: What kind of dog floats in the air?
A: An airedale.

Q: What do you get if an airedale floats too near the sun?
A: A hot dog.

Q: Why shouldn't you go up in the sky during a heavy storm?

A: Because it's already overclouded.

Q: What's the hardest storm to sweep up?

A: A dust storm.

Q: How do old storms travel fast?

A: They use hurrycanes.

Q: What's the difference between a thunderstorm and a sore lion?

A: One pours with rain while the other roars with pain.

Q: Why did the trees bow?
A: Because the thunder clapped.

Q: What knocks down houses and makes people laugh?
A: A cy-clown.

Q: Who is the king of winter?
A: Old King Cold.

Q: What does Old King Cold do?
A: He rains.

Q: Where does Old King Cold live?
A: Castles in the air.

Q: What do you get if you put a mousetrap in your freezer?
A: A cold snap.

Q: What do cats like to do in the winter?
A: Go mice skating.

Q: What can you catch if you go ice fishing?
A: You can catch cold.

Q: Why do windows have panes?
A: Because the rain beats on them.

Q: What do you get if you're hit by an icicle?
A: A cold sore.

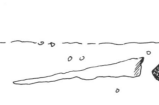

Q: What do you get when you cross a
snowstorm with a cornfield?
A: Cornflakes.

Q: Why do snow shovelers make a lot
of money?
A: Because there's no business like snow
business.

Q: What do you find in a snowbank?
A: Cold cash.

Q: How can animals tell what the weather's
going to be like?
A: They look at the furcast.

Q: How do bears know when winter is over and they can quit hibernating?

A: They look at their bear-ometer.

ABOUT THE AUTHORS

Rick and Ann Walton love to read, travel, play guitar, study foreign languages, and write for children. Rick also collects books and writes music while Ann knits and does origami. They live in Provo, Utah, where Ann is a computer programmer and Rick is practicing to be a moose wrestler. They have two incredible children.

ABOUT THE ARTIST

Susan Slattery Burke loves to illustrate fun-loving characters, especially animals. To her, each of them has a personality all their own. Her satisfaction comes when the characters come to life for the reader. Susan lives in Minneapolis, Minnesota, with her husband, her dog, and her cat. She is a graduate of the University of Minnesota. Susan enjoys sculpting, travel, illustrating, entertaining, and being outdoors.

You Must Be Joking

Alphabatty: Riddles from A to Z
Help Wanted: Riddles about Jobs
Here's to Ewe: Riddles about Sheep
Hide and Shriek: Riddles about
    Ghosts and Goblins
Ho Ho Ho! Riddles about Santa Claus
I Toad You So: Riddles about Frogs
    and Toads
On with the Show: Show Me Riddles
Out on a Limb: Riddles about Trees
    and Plants
That's for Shore: Riddles from
    the Beach
Weather or Not: Riddles for Rain
    and Shine
What's Gnu? Riddles from the Zoo
Wing It! Riddles about Birds